Threads & Friends

Book Four

Freddie the First Baseman Learns Gratitude

by Peter J. Mulry

NOW
PUBLISHING

1.888.5069-NOW
www.nowscpress.com
@nowscpress

Ordering Information:

Quantity sales. Special discounts are available on quantity purchases by corporations, associations, and others. For details, contact the publisher at the address above.

Orders by U.S. trade bookstores and wholesalers. Please contact: NOW SC Press: Tel: (888) 5069-NOW or visit www.nowscpress.com.

Printed in the United States of America

First Printing, 2018

ISBN: 978-1-7326611-7-2

I would like to thank several people who made this book possible - Lou Maggio, KR Lombardia, Gary Ippolito and Andy Taylor. I would also like to thank Mario Garcia, my Guardian Angel who has been with me through this endeavor. A tip of the cap to all the sponsors for their financial support.

Thanks to all who have helped me on my journey.

The All-Stars had practiced hard all week for their big game against the Wildcats. Freddie, the first baseman, had been putting in extra practice hours because he knew the Wildcats were a tough team, and hard to beat. He loved baseball, but he was kind of upset that all the practice time meant he couldn't hang out with his friends that much.

When he showed up on game day, he was grumpy. He did his warmup with his teammates, but started complaining before the first inning began. The weather was *too cold*, the bench *too hard*, the grass on the field *too long*. "Let's have a great game!" Coach Threads said.

"I guess so," Freddie grumbled as he walked to his position at first base.

The Wildcats were a good team, and by the fifth inning, they had scored five runs. The All-Stars only had one. Freddie walked into the dugout and hung his head. "They might win," he said to Gary, who played third base.

Gary shrugged. "As long as we play our hardest and do our best, that's still okay. Nobody wins all the time."

The game didn't improve for the All-Stars. By the time the ninth inning ended, the All-Stars lost, 9-2. The team lined up, opposite the Wildcats, for the traditional post-game handshake. Coach Threads had taught everyone that being respectful to the other teams, whether they won or lost, was just as important as playing well.

Gary went ahead of Freddie and shook the hands of each of the Wildcats. "Good game," Gary said.

Pedro the pitcher did the same. He was sad that the All-Stars had lost, but he didn't let it show in his face. "Good game," he said to the Wildcats as he shook hands with them.

Freddie, however, just trudged along. He didn't put out his hand to shake, and he didn't say "Good game." He got off the field as soon as possible and started putting his gear in his bag.

"Freddie, why didn't you shake with the other team?" Coach Threads asked him.

"Because they beat us. By a lot. Why should I be nice to them?"

"It's important to have good manners, both on and off the field. When you say 'please' and 'thank you', or something as simple as 'good game', you tell the other person that you respect them and the work they did," Coach Threads said.

"I guess so." Freddie swung his bag onto his shoulder. "Can I go now?"

"Sure. But I want you to think about what I said." Coach Threads handed Freddie a water bottle from the cooler. "See you at practice tomorrow."

When Freddie went home, he was still in a bad mood. His mother got mad at him for not saying "thank you" when his grandmother gave him a new sweatshirt. His father lectured him about saying "please" when asking his brother to share his video game. Freddie was sent to bed early for not being polite. After he put on his pajamas, he thought about what Coach had said.

Before their next game, Cathy the catcher had brought brownies for the whole team. They were chocolate with frosting and little red and white sprinkles on top, just like the team colors. Freddie went up to Cathy and put out his hand. "Where's mine?"

"Is that how we ask people to share, Freddie?" Coach Threads said.

Freddie frowned, and tried again. "Can I have mine, please?"

Cathy handed him a brownie. "Here you go. I decorated yours with a little number one, for first base."

Freddie was about to take a bite, when he saw Coach looking at him. "Thank you, Cathy," Freddie said. "That was very nice of you."

She gave him a big smile. "You're welcome."

This game went better than the last one, but in the end, the All-Stars lost again, 7-6. The other team lined up across from the All-Stars and shook their hands. Freddie knew several of the players from school and from his neighborhood. The Cougars' first baseman was in Freddie's class at school, and often rode the same bus.

When Freddie stopped beside the Cougars' first baseman, he put out his hand and shook with him. The Cougars' player lived two doors down from Freddie and was a really strong first baseman. "Good game. You made some great throws."

"Thank you," the other boy said. "You catch really well, though. It was a close game, because you guys are a great team."

Freddie loved playing baseball, and he loved learning how to be better at his position. "Do you think maybe we could practice throwing and catching after school?" Freddie asked, then he added, "please?"

"That sounds like a great idea!" the other boy said. "How about tomorrow? We can have ice cream at my house afterwards."

After the handshake, Coach Threads pulled Freddie aside. "I appreciate you being respectful to the other team, and to Cathy earlier. I bet that brownie tasted even better, because you were nice to her and appreciative."

Freddie thought about it. The snack had been extra yummy, and it had been nice to see Cathy smile when he thanked her. "It was."

"I noticed you talking to the first baseman for the other team," Coach said.

Freddie nodded. "He said he could teach me some of those great throws he did, if I help him with catching."

"That's really nice of you, Freddie." Coach Threads smiled. "I'm proud of you for being so respectful to the other team."

"I didn't want to be," Freddie admitted, "because I don't like to lose. But they were a strong team, and in the end, I made a new friend."

"And you're going home not so grumpy this time?"

Freddie grinned. It did feel good to make other people smile, and to tell them he appreciated them. "Definitely. I can't wait to practice after school tomorrow."

"Good job." Coach Threads gathered the team around and gave them all a thumbs-up. "You all played hard out there, and I'm proud of you for being polite and respectful to the Wildcats. The All-Stars might not win every game, but we're going to be winners in life. In the long run, it's not about the games, it's about the person you become."

The team cheered. When Freddie turned to leave,
he stopped beside Coach Threads. "Thank you,
Coach. For everything."

The smile on Coach's face warmed Freddie's heart.
"You're very welcome, Freddie." And when Freddie
went home that day, he was smiling, too.

Freddie

the 1st Baseman

Freddie's Baseball Skills on the Field

☆ When covering first base, put your heels on each corner of the base and be able to reach out for the ball

☆ Learn how to use first baseman's mitt. It makes many ground ball plays easier

☆ Catch & throw from cut-off man position

☆ Cover bunts when the situation calls for it

Correct Choices — Freddie's Life Skills on the Field

Perception - Be aware of every situation on every pitch

Comprehension - Understand the game situation and pay attention

Action - Know what to do on each play & do it

Manners - Know the "Do's & Don'ts" of the game. It's baseball etiquette

Look for the other books in the
Threads & Friends series!

Teamwork

Book One

Threads & The All-Star Team

Cathy the Catcher's New View

Pedro the Pitcher's Second Chance

Turn the page for an

excerpt from...

Cathy the Catcher's New View

Cathy the Catcher settled into her position behind the batter, gave her signal to Pedro the pitcher, and watched Pedro wind up to throw a curveball. Cathy put up her glove. The batter swung and missed, the ball rushed past him, bounced off the backstop and landed on the dirt behind home plate. Cathy scrambled to pick it up and throw it back to Pedro. "Sorry!"

She got back into position and signaled for another curveball. They were down by two runs in the third inning, but they already had two outs against the other team. One more, and her All-Stars team would have a chance to close that gap. Pedro leaned back, pitched, and the ball whizzed through the air. The batter swung again, missed. Cathy reached with her glove—

And missed again. The ball bounced off the tip of her glove and hit the backstop a second time. When she went to pick up the ball, she could feel her teammates staring at her. Her cheeks flushed as she threw the ball back to Pedro. He stepped to the right, but the ball was too far outside his reach. Gary ran over from third base, picked up the ball and gave it to Pedro.

By the fourth inning, Cathy had missed more balls than she caught. Tears burned her eyes. She rubbed them with the back of her fist, but her vision blurred. She was usually a pretty good catcher. What was wrong today? Pedro came running up and gave Cathy a pat on the back. "Don't worry. You're just having an off day."

Coach Threads pulled Cathy aside after the game. "You seem to be struggling, Cathy. Is everything all right?"

"Yeah, I guess," she said.

"As the catcher, you're accountable for making sure the pitcher delivers the right pitch, and that you are ready to catch the ball at all times," Coach Threads said. "The catcher is a very important position. If you need help or extra practice, you need to speak up. Okay?"

She nodded and went home, telling herself it was just an *off* day, as Pedro said. But Cathy's off day turned into an off week. She couldn't seem to catch the ball, and at school, she missed writing down two assignments and had trouble understanding the math problem her teacher demonstrated on the whiteboard. Her head hurt almost every day but she tried not to complain. At the end of the day, baseball practice was usually her favorite time, but not today. Cathy trudged into the locker room.

Name:

Team:

Position:

Baseball Skills on the field:

Life Skills on the field:

About the Author

Pete Mulry, one of the winningest coaches in high school baseball, coached for ten years at Tampa Catholic High School, and left that job with an overall high school record of 329-39. His team won State Championships in '68, '71, '73, and '76 and a National Championship in '73. He was honored as Florida Coach of the year in 1968, 1971, 1973 and 1976 and Nominated for National Coach of the year in 1977. Pete then moved on to the collegiate level, coaching the University of Tampa from 1978  through 1982. He also scouted for KC Royals. He was recently honored by the *Tampa Tribune* as one of the Top 50 Coaches in athletics in the Tampa Bay area. He has dedicated his life, and his foundation, the Peter J. Mulry Foundation, to teach young children life skills through sports.